HOW TO WIN AGAINST STUDENT LOANS

Andre Edwards

ISBN: 979-8-9875007-1-2

DEDICATION

This book is dedicated to my mother for giving me the keys to education.

This book is dedicated to those who want more in life. Don't stop dreaming, keep pushing against the norm of settling for what life has dealt you.

AFFILIATE DISCLAIMER

The short, direct, non-legal version is this: Some of the links in this report may be affiliate links which means that I earn money if you choose to buy from that vendor at some point in the near future. I do not choose which products and services to promote based upon which pay me the most, I choose based upon my decision of which I would recommend to a dear friend. You will never pay more for an item by clicking through my affiliate link

DISCLAIMER AND/OR LEGAL NOTICES

The information presented herein represents the view of the author as of the date of publication. Because of the rate with which conditions change, the author reserves the right to alter and update his opinion based on the new conditions. The report is for informational purposes only. While every attempt has been made to verify the information provided in this report, neither the author nor his affiliates/partners assume any responsibility for errors, inaccuracies or omissions. Any slights of people or organizations are unintentional. If advice concerning legal or related matters is needed, the services of a fully qualified professional should be sought. This report is not intended for use as a source of legal or accounting advice. You should be aware of any laws which govern business transactions or other business practices in your country and state. Any reference to any person or business whether living or dead is purely coincidental. The author obtained the information contained herein from sources he believes to be reliable and from his own personal experience, but neither implies nor intends any guarantee of accuracy. The author particularly disclaims any liability, loss, or risk taken by individuals who directly or indirectly act on the information contained herein. The author believes the advice presented here is sound, but reader cannot hold him responsible for either the actions they take or indirectly act on the information contained herein.

TABLE OF CONTENTS

INTRODUCTION

Are you struggling to make ends meet while paying off your student loans? Do you feel overwhelmed and stressed out by the amount of debt you have from your student loans? Are you tired of feeling like your student loans are holding you back from achieving your financial goals?

If you answered yes to any of these questions, then this book is for you. In the following pages, you will discover a proven strategy for paying off your student loans faster than ever thought possible. With practical tips and actionable advice, you will learn how to make the most of your income, set realistic goals, and stay motivated even when the going gets tough.

I am Andre Edwards, a native of Jamaica, but I grew up in Washington DC. I graduated from DC Public Schools. I then matriculated through the University of Pittsburgh, where I received my Bachelor's in Social work and Psychology and then my Master's Degree in Social work and Mental health. I did not have a scholarship so my mother had to pay for tuition. Between my Bachelor's and Master's degree, I accrued about $58,000.00 worth of student loan debt. Now that's not an easy number to digest coming out of college, as a young person. As a recent graduate, you may feel financially overwhelmed and find it difficult to achieve independence. You're entering the job market, trying to secure a stable income while also managing expenses like car payments and rent. Student loans can add to the stress and make it challenging to stay afloat. But by taking control of your finances and prioritizing debt repayment, you can set yourself up for a brighter future.

Student loans can feel like a heavy burden, a ball and chain that requires monthly payments. If you fall behind, the debt can quickly balloon and become even harder to manage. It's a constant challenge to keep up with these payments and still achieve financial independence, but it's not impossible.

When I was paying off my student loans, myself, my wife, and my toddler were sharing one bedroom. So I had a lot of incentive to change our situation by paying off our student loans. Paying off my student loans has made a world of difference.

You can also change your situation by freeing yourself up from student debt. Imagine what you could do if you made the decision to pay off your student loan. How would it change your quality of life? This book is designed to help you pay off your student loans and take control of your finances. By sharing my experience and the strategies that worked for me, I want to empower you to achieve financial freedom and build the life you want.

So if you're in the process of earning your bachelor's or master's degree, are a new graduate, or just desire to pay off your student loan, in this book, I will show you how to pay off your student loans with an easy strategy. My solution framework offers practical tips on managing finances, setting goals, and remaining motivated in your repayment process. It offers positive insights of being debt-free and empowers readers with strategies to remove student loan debt on their journey toward financial freedom. The common mistakes that people make while implementing this solution are ignoring their student debt, making minimum payments, neglecting their budget and giving up. Here is the first thing that you should do.

CHAPTER 1

LEARN AND KNOW THAT PAYBACK IS POSSIBLE

When you're going to pay off your student loans, search for people who have already paid off their loans. Look for examples of people that have paid off significant amounts of debt that they owed to lenders. You can find these people on YouTube, and on the internet. I searched Google and Yahoo for people who have paid off their student loans. Examples motivate you to say, "Oh, wow. This is actually possible". Through these examples, you will learn that you don't have to live with your student loans forever.

It was an accident that I found out that paying off your student loans early was even possible. I applied to an income driven student loan forgiveness program, and I paid it faithfully. I was very consistent with that program as it drafted monies from my bank account. I was paying about $200.00 plus dollars a month toward my student loan. I monitored the balance of the student loan and after a year and a half, I noticed that the balance of the loan was not decreasing. I thought "okay, well, at least they're off my back," and I just kept the payment agreement going. It took a drastic change in my checking account for me to notice that the income-based agreement had actually expired. As a result, my payment tripled from $200.00 plus dollars to about $643.00 dollars. Because of this change in payment, I learned that the balance subsequently decreased payment.

Sometimes we have moments of revelation, and that's exactly what happened to me. I realized that if I made additional payments towards my student loan, the balance would decrease faster. It was empowering to discover a way to take control of my debt and make progress towards financial freedom. I learned that I can decrease the principal and total monies owed to my loan over time.

What is the Benefit of Paying Off Your Student Loans?

In 2013, I desired to get a house and improve my finances. My **strategy was to get my student debt paid off, because that $643.00 plus payment a month weakened the probability of acquiring a house. Getting rid of student loan debt can provide a tremendous sense of relief and alleviate financial** stress. It's a weight off your shoulders, allowing you to focus on other goals and priorities without the constant burden of debt hanging over you.

I learned that money and your mental health are inextricably linked. Especially if you're a provider, I know it's hard to think through anxiety and worry when your personal finances are strained.

I also learned that once you pay off your student loan debt, your money can be invested in assets. Maybe you can apply it to the downpayment of your first home or investment property, maybe it will go to your stock portfolio. Once you get your student loans out of the way you can build your wealth, and focus on things that matter such as your health and relationships.

Do you have any other benefits that you can add here?:

_____

_____

_____

_____

_____

Make A Decision

Early on in my student loan journey, I was not serious about paying my student debt and negotiated paying the minimum amount of money to keep my lenders at bay. I couldn't continue with my old behavior, I had to make a life changing decision. I remember the day I was in my workplace parking lot, the thought hit me like a lightning bolt. There was a compelling feeling to change my behavior due to the pending growth of my family.

Paying off your student loans is a critical decision that can have a profound impact on your future. Student loan debt cannot be discharged from credit reports and cannot be claimed in bankruptcy - it's a debt that you must take charge of and eliminate. So, what's your reason for paying off your student loan? Maybe you want to achieve financial freedom, pursue your dream career, or start a family. Whatever your reason, by taking action now, you're setting yourself up for a brighter future and greater peace of mind.

You have the power to take control of your finances and make a decision to pay off your student loans. Don't wait for tomorrow or some distant future - the time to act is now. By making this choice, you're setting yourself up for a more secure financial future, and you'll be better prepared for whatever life throws your way.

Write your reason to pay off your student loan:

_____

_____

_____

_____

_____

The Keys Within the Process

Students loans are not dischargeable and one cannot claim bankruptcy to remove them from your credit file. There may be special circumstances to instantly erase these loans but most of us can take the steps below. Here are the steps you can take to pay off your student loan, based on the strategy I have used.

Action Steps:

1. Make a decision to Pay Off your loans. Saying "yes" will begin your payoff journey and open opportunities to you.

2. Find examples of persons who have paid their student debt using web searches, and Youtube. This will yield thousands of results. Type this content into your search bar to help adjust your personal algorithm.

3. Take Action.

CHAPTER 2

PLAN YOUR SAVINGS WITH YOUR CALENDAR

Plan your savings using Google Calendar. Build your goals 6 months to one year out within Google Calendar or a calendar of your choice. Set clear expectations and mark specific calendar dates every two weeks, where you write down and affirm, "I will have a certain amount of money in my savings account." The calendar will automatically give you reminders of where you should be within your savings. Write down your goals, because when you write down your goals and you can see your goals, you are exponentially more likely to achieve them rather than just keeping them within your head. Keep your goals in front of you!

Use specific, measurable, achievable, relatable, and timely goals or SMART goals. Here is an example "I have saved $1000.00 by September,2023." Specificity and keeping your goals within a window of time will help you execute your goals.

These goals were the foundation of my plan student loan payoff. And within your plan, you should have goals too, stick to this strategy.

Visualize Your Outcome

Visualize paying off your student loans. Elite athletes do this before they perform in their events to win. You may not be an athlete but paying off your student loans can be an Olympic task. Use your abilities to sense, imagine, feel and think (SIFT). Utilize your five senses to vividly experience the day when you successfully pay off your loans. Imagine and see yourself writing your last check to the loan vendor; if you have challenges with this use a visual aid such as a vision board. Feel your emotions after your last payment: are you elated, happy, relieved or joyful? What thoughts are you thinking after you pay your student loan off? This is a very powerful strategy that you can use a few minutes daily to help you achieve your goal. If you believe it, you must see it in your mind first.

Action Steps:

1. Find a quiet space and SIFT toward your payoff outcome. Use all of your senses to see and feel receiving your Pay Off letter.

2. Write down your goals, add them to your phone calendar. Create short and long term SMART goals to approach your target.

CHAPTER 3

PAY WHILE SAVING

Pay yourself first. When you see your student loan decreasing, while your bank savings are increasing, this will multiply your personal morale. Set up an automatic draft from your checking account to your savings account for your scheduled pay days. Increase the amount of savings as your pay increases as well. If you are in the position where you can ask for a pay raise or can acquire another professional licensure that will increase your income, go for it. Continue to add any monetary increase to your financial cushion.

If you do not feel that you can save money and pay down your student, I suggest starting with small contributions to your savings. It may feel like a stretch to you but it can be done. First, start with small contributions to your savings to develop the confidence over time to save more. Gradually increase your increments of money saved over time until you feel comfortable. The tactic to save while paying will require you to spend less of your income while also increasing take home earnings.

It took me about five years to complete my loan payoff process. You may be thinking five years is too much time. If I didn't do it, five years would have passed anyway and the difference would have been whether I paid my student loans off or not. What is 5 years of focus and planning, versus regret about not making the decision(s) to eliminate student for the rest of your life? According to www.educationdata.org, the average college graduate takes 20 years to pay off their student debt. So wherever you're at in your personal life or age, consider how long you want to take to remain committed to student debt versus committing to a better future when you partner with intention.

Avoid Lifestyle Creep: Increased Earnings, Same Lifestyle

According to PEW research about 32 percent of college graduates move back home to live with their parents. If you are in this position, delayed gratification can help you. Meaning, resist moving from your parents home. Save more money by not having to pay market rent and delay making large purchase's such as a home. Your financial cushion can become bigger while living at your parents home but this first requires goal planning.

If you're at a job or a place of employment where they increase your salary overtime, save the increase and live the same, don't change your lifestyle. Meaning resist buying the latest car or possessions that may lose value overtime. You may feel tempted to buy more pricey possessions because your wages have increased but resist this temptation. Also, be mindful that your wage increase is a cost of living adjustment to help keep up with inflation. For example an employer may increase your wage by 2 percent but US inflation increased 2 percent in the same year. Inflation means that your purchasing power decreases, please be aware of this.

Notice and take advantage of adjustments in your market such as gas prices as well. If in your area, the gas price goes down, save that difference. Pay attention to the little things like this, the money does add up. Focusing on the use of additional funds toward student loan repayment will contribute to building a solid financial foundation. . Rerouting money back into your personal economy will give you a sense of power over your finances.

Automate Your Monthly Payment

Automate your monthly payments to your student loan lender, authorize your lender to draft monthly payments from your bank account. Ask your lender if they offer this option. You can benefit and receive a discount because of the automatic drafts, so sign-up for this through your lender. I did this and my loan interest rate was reduced by 0.25%. This strategy, if offered, can potentially save you thousands.

Apply Your Savings

Finally, accumulate money or savings to apply to your student loans and then schedule your payments. **Never drain/empty your savings account to pay off your student loans**.

I scheduled my payments and made sure they were applied to the loan balance. I applied big payments, then I waited at least two days to see if the payment applied to the loan. If the payment made a difference, then I applied another. For example, if you are enrolled in a loan forgiveness program, such as Public Service Loan Forgiveness (PSLF) or Income-Driven Repayment (IDR) forgiveness, making extra payments may not provide a substantial benefit. In these programs, your remaining loan balance is forgiven after a certain number of qualifying payments, typically 10 or 20 years. Additional payments may not accelerate forgiveness. Also read the terms of your Private or Federal loans when repaying. This information also helped me to avoid disappointment by making sure that payments were applied to the principal amount

Action Steps:

1. Setup an automatic bank draft, transferring monies from your checking to savings account. Schedule these drafts for your paydays.

2. Ask about an automatic debit by your student loan lender . If the automatic debit reduces your interest rate, take advantage of this.

3. Increase savings over time to add to your savings account. Keep personal consumption low as your pay increases.

4. Pursue certifications and licensures that help to increase your total income. This helps you long term in your professional life to then pay off student loans.

CHAPTER 4

PART TIME GIG

It's not just the debt problem that we have in America in respect to student loans. It's also an income problem as well. I suggest earning more by doing more. Consider a home based business, or become a part time contractor. There are many other ways to earn additional income in this economy, including rideshare or being a delivery person. Utilize this gig economy and acquire part time work to supplement your nine to five job income. Focus on achieving a specific financial goal by the end of your shift, whether that is making an extra $50 to $100 a day. Maybe you can work your gig five to six days out of the week. If you can achieve $100 a day at 6 days a week this will gross about $2,400.00 a month. Your gig work is only for a short and planned period of time, remain consistent to hit your financial bottom line. It definitely makes a big income difference over time, but have an exit plan.

The key is being very aggressive toward student debt. Because debt will remain if you do not strategize and become aggressive.

I have utilized opportunities to help repay my student loan. These opportunities also have an additional benefit of improving your resilience, confidence and problem solving skills. Here are 3 Opportunities as an independent contractor that can potentially yield you additional income on a part time basis:

1. Rideshare Driving
2. Food Delivery Driving
3. Network Marketing

Stick to Your Plan

As of 2022 close to 43 million Americans have federal student loans. US borrowers owe a combined $1.8 trillion in student loan debt as of October 2022, but you don't have to be in that number anymore. It all starts with a grasp of understanding your financial situation. Know how much money you are earning and spending. What are you spending on rent/mortgage, utilities, and luxury?

Remain committed to your plan in challenging circumstances. I lost my job in 2018, but I had to stick with my plan During that challenging time, I had to dip into my savings and explore additional income opportunities to meet my obligations. I eventually regained full employment, it's a testament to the importance of perseverance and adaptability. You just have to keep moving toward your accumulation of income.

Action Steps:

1. Increase your income. Find an opportunity to bring in extra cash. Create a weekly and monthly income goal.

2. Stick to your plan. Continue to remain focused on the outcome of paying off your student debt.

CHAPTER 5

ADJUST YOUR W-4

This is not financial advice but please consider adjusting your W-4. Change your W-4 allowances to increase net take home income. I am part of a family of three and I was able to adjust my allowances appropriately. This increased my bi-weekly income and I contributed those extra funds back to my savings. I have included a resource in regards to the W-4 within the resource section of this book. Also consult with a tax professional to adjust your W-4 accordingly.

Apply Tax Refund(s)

When you receive your annual tax refunds, allocate a portion to pay off your student loans. This additional allocation can save you thousands of dollars and time paying back student loans and will improve your overall financial health. Using your tax refund is a great boost but continue to maintain your regular monthly payments.

Consolidate Your Loans

I consolidated my loan payments to simplify repayment. I combined my loans to become a single loan therefore allowing me to have one monthly payment. This can increase your organization about paying your student loans and paying them back in a timely matter. Consolidating your loans may lower your overall interest rate and potentially lower your monthly payment because the loan term can be extended. This can offer more wiggle room with your budget. A fixed interest rate can help you save throughout the time of a consolidated loan, allowing you to better predict how to manage your budget and guard against increases in interest rates.

Ask a Lawyer

Did you know that you can ask a lawyer about student loans. If you have legal questions about lenders, debt consolidation, or your rights as a loan borrower. A lawyer can help you negotiate terms with your lender as well. You can contact an attorney about this. I utilized an attorneys consultation to help strategize the pay back of my student loan. I have included an affordable resource in the resource section for you.

Action Steps:

1. Ask your Human Resources about the W-4 Form. Consult reputable sources on how to adjust your W-4 appropriately. I have included one resource within the resource section of this book.

2. Reserve a portion of your tax refunds to pay your student debt. Adding additional payments will reduce your balance and interest earned on your debt.

CHAPTER 6

PAY ATTENTION

Review your student loans on a continuous basis(weekly or biweekly) to make sure your loan balance is decreasing in real time. This will build morale to get closer to ultimately paying off your student loans. The key is really **paying attention to the principal and interest in respect to your student loans.**

Check Your Loan Schedule

You should check the amortization schedule of your student loan, you could ask for this item from your lenders customer service department. You may also be able to find this item when you log into your personal online lender account. The amortization schedule will show month by month, the balance of the loan as you pay off your student loan. It will show you the principal and the interest owed. This tool will provide you with a clear and accurate picture of your progress over time, serving as a reliable map to help guide you in paying off your student loan. So know the numbers in respect to your loan term length, my own was about twenty years. Know your interest rate (my rate was about 6.25%) . If you're paying $600.00 a month or more per student loan, how much of your money is going toward interest and how much is going into principal? Consider that if you're paying $600.00 per month, $200.00 may be going towards your principal and $400.00 going towards interest. Awareness will make the difference of you paying or saving thousands of dollars in the life of your student debt. In my experience I saved myself about $80,728 by getting ahead of my loan amortization schedule. You might want to keep this within your radar and use it as a guide(I have included a loan calculator in the resource section also).

Also consider refinancing your student loan. Check with your lender to learn if this is an option to reduce the interest from your debt. Reducing your interest rate will help adjust the ratio between principal and interest, saving you thousands of dollars in the long run.

Pay Back Programs

If you can, avoid income based pay back programs. The reason being is because I noticed my loan balance increasing when paying the minimum to lenders. I paid only interest when using the income based program. It was not serving me any benefit, and it won't serve you any benefit if you just pay the minimum with some of these programs. . It was a blessing that the loan program agreement actually expired in my case. This was a catalyst and inspiration to start doing more about paying off my debt. This gave me the gas and momentum to start being aggressive with my student loans knowing that there was a hope to be able to actually pay it down when increasing the monthly payment.

Track Your Spending, Find Your Money

One of the things you may want to do to reach your financial goals is limit eating out. If you are buying meals at a restaurant this adds up, buy groceries, and make several meals out of your groceries. Quit going to your favorite food spot at lunchtime(as I did), because all that cash can be returned to your bank account. For instance, if you average spending $10.00 per meal, when you go out for lunch, you multiply that by five days a work week, that's $50.00. Continue this behavior for four weeks and that results in $200.00 a month spent. Take that $200.00 a month, multiplied by 12 months, that's $2,400.00 a year. This $2,400.00 can go back into your account. Additionally consider subscriptions such as your cell phone carrier. Is your current cell phone service the most affordable? Also, consider minimizing subscriptions to streaming services and cable. These seemingly small fees for streaming services can add up in addition to cable services. Research your employers perks if these perks can be applied to services that you are currently using, this can potentially save you money.

If you have car insurance, ask if they have any discounts for customers. I found a discount by signing up for my car insurance's programs. Remain open to switching car insurance which has fluctuating premiums from year to year. If it costs you $10.00 dollars per day to park in your jobs parking lot, but public parking is free, consider switching to public parking for a period of time.

What are alternative methods to discover additional funds? Write this below:

_____

_____

_____

_____

_____

Do the math. Stick with a plan and be flexible. Also, I alluded to the hard truth of paying more than what you are asked for. When you're paying back more, you are decreasing that principal amount, you're also decreasing the amount of additional interest paid over time. Resist paying only the minimum on your student loans to keep them at bay.

Action Steps:

1. Create an online account through your lenders website. You will be able see payment activity within your account. You can now see how payment is applied to principal and interest.

2. Stop or limit eating at food establishments because the accumulation of these meals is costing you hundreds a month to thousands a year. Take lunch to work for 1 month and notice the immediate difference within your savings. These savings can be used for additional payments to your debt.

3. Remain flexible and curious. Call your lender to learn if there are options to refinance to a lower interest rate.

CONCLUSION

I was scheduled to pay off my student loan by 2025. I paid off my student loan in early 2020, because I committed to a decision and timeline.

I lost my employment in my process so I had to remain flexible and use the money I saved as a cushion. Do not interpret delay as denial when life events happen to you. Life and finances tend to respond well when you have a plan. Just make sure your plan keeps you on the path of paying off your student loans.

What I've shared within this book is a process that you can borrow elements, strategies, and tips from. . You will thank yourself over and over for making a decision and taking action to change your future. You can and will win!

RESOURCES

Calculate your loan schedule here
https://www.calculator.net/student-loan-calculator.html

Research information about the W-4
https://www.irs.gov/forms-pubs/about-form-w-4

Can Student loans be discharged?
https://www.experian.com/blogs/ask-experian/can-bankruptcy-get-rid-of-student-loans/

Get Legal Advice
Afjustice.info

Student Loan Sates
https://nces.ed.gov/fastfacts/display.asp?id=900

Rules for When Your Graduate Moves Back Home After College
https://www.cnb.com/personal-banking/insights/moving-back-home-after-college.html#:~:text=Moving%20back%20in%20with%20mom,parents%2C%20according%20to%20Pew%20Research.

Average Time to Repay Student Loans
https://educationdata.org/average-time-to-repay-student-loans